Jack Campbell

THE BACON COOKBOOK

Scratch + Sniff

Smith Street Books

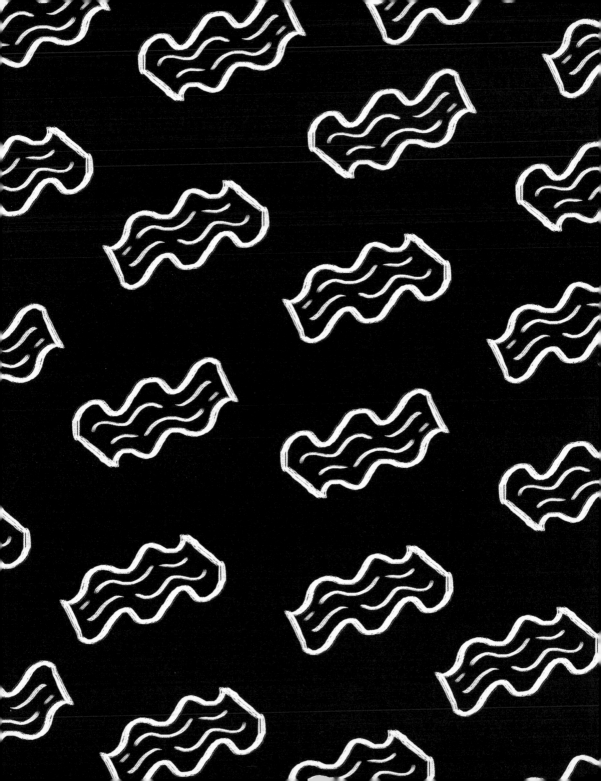

Contents

Introduction

It's an indisputable fact that bacon is the world's greatest food. It goes with everything – from savoury to sweet – and it's just as comfortable being the star of the show as it is playing a supporting role. You can slather it in maple syrup; you can fry it 'til it's crisp; you can use it to wrap other meats; hell, you can even weave a delicious bacony mat with it, and bacon confidently takes it all in its stride. All hail bacon.

SO, WHAT IS BACON?

Aside from being a miraculous ingredient that can do almost anything, bacon is a cured meat product made from a pig. It can be dry-cured, where it's packed in salt, or wet-cured in brine (which is a magical solution of salt and water). Preservatives are also used at this stage, both in commercial and home curing – the most common being sodium nitrate and sodium nitrite, which also gives bacon its pinky colouring. Sugar and additional flavours can also be added to the cure, such as pepper, garlic, bourbon, vanilla, maple syrup, bay leaves, and so on. Once the meat is cured, you've got bacon. It doesn't have to be smoked (some bacon is just air dried), but I think we can all agree that it's much much better when it is. A variety of woods can be used to impart different flavours, including hickory, apple, mesquite, maple, peach and pecan.

CUTS OF BACON

STREAKY BACON

Also known as 'side' or 'belly' bacon, this cut is the one most commonly found in the US. Streaky bacon is made from the belly, and is so called as the meat is streaked with quite a lot of fat, making it a great choice if you like your bacon cooked crispy and crunchy.

LOIN BACON

Also known as 'back', 'collar' or 'Canadian' bacon, loin is a much leaner, meatier cut which comes from the middle of the back of the pig. This is the cut most commonly found in the UK.

MIDDLE BACON

Probably most common in Australia, this cut includes both the loin and a long strip of the belly – the best of both worlds!

BUYING BACON

Like most foods, there's a huge range when it comes to quality. And again, like most foods, bacon that's produced with a bit of love and care and transparency is generally of higher quality than stuff that's been mass-produced. Look for bacon made from free-range pigs that comes from smaller producers, ideally someone local. If you're buying packaged bacon, avoid anything that looks too processed and check the ingredients - if the list reminds you more of a high school chemistry exam than your breakfast, it's probably better back on the shelf.

Most bacon is sold pre-sliced, often with the skin, or rind, already removed. If you're a bacon fiend, why not consider purchasing a whole slab? You can slice it as thickly (or thinly) as you want and - I cannnot stress this benefit enough - you will have a *whole slab* of bacon in your fridge. It can also be a more economical way to buy it, and the bacon will keep for longer if it's uncut.

Get out there and try a few different types to see what you like. You may prefer maple-infused thick-cut loin bacon or hickory-smoked streaky bacon sliced super thin (who are we kidding, we know you love both). The point is, there's no need to restrict yourself to just one type of bacon.

MAKING YOUR OWN BACON

This is 100 per cent guaranteed to make you the coolest person in the world. All you need is the dry cure recipe below and the Bacon from scratch recipe on the next page, and you won't be bringin' home the bacon, you'll be making it right there at home like a boss, while the mere mortals around you just look on in awe and amazement.

BASIC DRY CURE

Pink curing salt can be ordered online or is available at butchers' supply shops. Also known as pink salt, Prague powder number 1, insta cure #1 and sel rose, curing salt contains sodium nitrite which is crucial to the curing process. Not to be confused with Himalayan or Murray River salt - these salts are pink, but they won't bring you bacon.

Makes enough for about 3 slabs of bacon

120 g (4½ oz) salt

60 g (2 oz) caster sugar

14 g (½ oz/2 teaspoons) pink curing salt #1

Combine the salt, sugar and pink salt in a bowl and mix well. Store in an airtight container indefinitely.

Nothing beats making your own bacon. Try to source ethically raised pork from your local farmers' market or butcher. Ask for the thickest end of the belly. Bacon is traditionally smoked to give it a distinctive flavour, but not everyone has the equipment to pull that off. Cooking in a low oven is simple and still results in that bacon magic.

MAKES 1 SLAB BACON – ABOUT 1.8 KG (4 LB)

2.2 kg (4 lb 14 oz) piece boneless skin-on pork belly, trimmed so the edges are square

70 g (2½ oz/¼ cup) dry cure (see page 7)

125 ml (4 fl oz/½ cup) pure maple syrup

NOTE: IF THE BACON IS TOO SALTY, BLANCH IN SIMMERING WATER FOR 60 SECONDS AND DRAIN WELL BEFORE COOKING.

Choose an airtight non-reactive container or a zip-lock bag just large enough to hold the pork. (It's important that the container or bag is a close fit to the size of the pork, as the salty cure liquid and the moisture that is released from the pork needs to surround the meat and remain in contact with it as much as possible.)

Spread the dry cure in the container or pour into the bag. Press all sides of the belly into the cure to give it an even coating all over, or place in the bag and turn the bag gently to coat in the cure. Add the maple syrup and turn the pork until coated. Refrigerate the belly for 7 days, turning the meat or bag every day to redistribute the cure liquid. After 7 days, check the belly for firmness. If it feels firm at its thickest point, it is cured and ready. If the meat feels slightly soft, cure for a further day or two.

Preheat the oven to 75°C/165°F (fan-forced) or prepare a hot smoker following the manufacturer's instructions. Line a large roasting pan with baking paper or foil and place a wire rack on top. Remove the belly from the cure and discard the liquid. Rinse the belly well and pat dry with paper towel. Roast or smoke for 1½–2 hours or until the internal temperature reaches 65°C (150°F).

Remove the pork from the oven or smoker and carefully remove the skin with a small, sharp knife, keeping the blade as close to the skin as possible and peeling it back as you go. Discard the skin. Set the bacon aside to cool, wrap well and refrigerate until required. Slice with a very sharp, long thin knife as required.

The bacon will store well wrapped in the refrigerator for 1–2 weeks. Or you can cut into slices, lardons or small chunks and wrap in portions, then freeze for up to 3 months.

How to create a bacon weave

Also known as a 'bacon lattice', the bacon weave makes for the ultimate sandwich or burger filling that delivers the perfect amount of bacon with every bite.

NOTE: THIS LARGE WEAVE USES 16 SLICES OF MIDDLE (LONG-CUT) BACON, BUT YOU CAN MAKE A SMALL WEAVE WITH JUST 6 SLICES. FOR A NICE EVEN END RESULT, TRY TO FIND BACON THAT'S FAIRLY UNIFORM IN SHAPE AND SIZE.

1. On a clean work surface or piece of baking paper, lay out your first set of vertical slices, leaving enough space between each for another slice of bacon.

2. Place one slice of bacon horizontally at the top over the vertical slices.

3. Lay out a second set of vertical slices on top of the horizontal slice, filling the space between the first set of slices.

4. Fold back the first set of vertical slices (the ones that are sitting beneath the horizontal slice).

5. Place another horizontal slice on top, ensuring it's nice and close to the folds.

6. Unfold the vertical slices so they sit over the second horizontal slice.

7. Fold back the second set of vertical slices, the ones that are now sitting below the second horizontal slice. Place a third horizontal slice on top, ensuring it's close to the folds, and then again, unfold the vertical slices. You will start to see the weave pattern emerging.

8-9. Repeat the previous steps, alternating between folding back the first and second sets of vertical slices, until you have a square woven mat of tasty, tasty bacon.

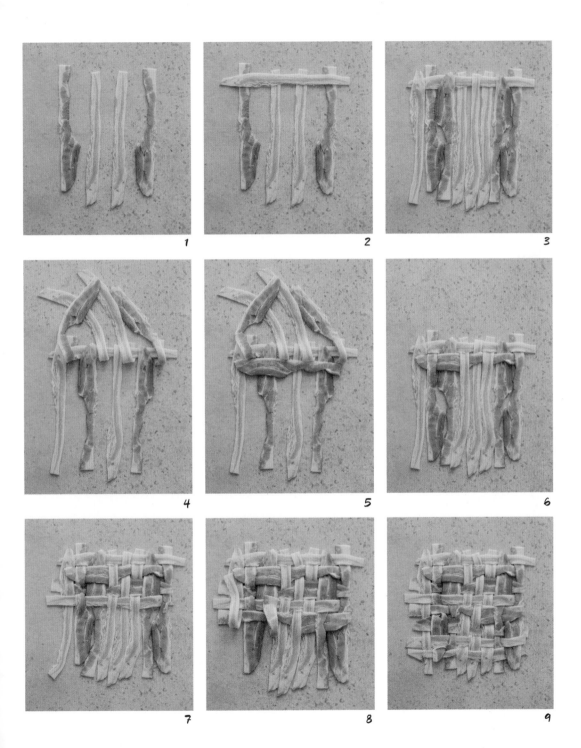

Honey caramel, bacon & macadamia popcorn

SERVES 8-10

2 tablespoons olive oil

125 g (4½ oz) rindless loin (back) bacon, diced

75 g (2¾ oz/⅓ cup) popping corn

3 tablespoons honey

150 g (5½ oz/⅔ cup) caster (superfine) sugar

125 g (4½ oz) unsalted butter, chopped

100 g (3½ oz/¾ cup) salted macadamia nuts, roughly chopped

Line a large baking tray with baking paper. Heat 2 teaspoons of the oil in a frying pan over medium–high heat and cook the bacon for 6–8 minutes, or until very well browned and crisp. Remove with a slotted spoon and drain on paper towel.

Pour the bacon fat from the pan, plus the remaining olive oil, into a large heavy-based saucepan and place over medium heat. After a minute or so test if the oil mixture is hot enough by adding a couple of grains of corn to the pan - they should spin slowly. Add the corn, shake the pan to coat in the oil mixture, and cover. Shake the pan regularly until the popping ceases. Remove from the heat and tip into a large heatproof bowl. Discard any unpopped corn and set the bowl aside.

Stir the honey, sugar and butter in a heavy-based saucepan over low heat until the sugar dissolves. Increase the heat to medium and boil for 4-5 minutes without stirring, or until the caramel is golden brown.

Remove from the heat, stir in the macadamia nuts and bacon, and pour over the popped corn. Working quickly, fold the mixture gently until the corn is well combined (a silicon spatula is really useful for this task). Spread over the prepared tray and set aside for 30 minutes or until cool and set. Break into pieces to serve.

Store in an airtight container in the refrigerator for 3-4 days (if there's any left by then).

NOTE: THIS POPCORN IS ALSO GREAT MADE WITH ROASTED SALTED PEANUTS INSTEAD OF MACADAMIA NUTS.

Crunchy, sweet, salty, bacony ... this popcorn is the ultimate movie snack or party food. It also makes a great gift, but someone would have to pry it out of your greedy little hands first.

Candied
bacon

Sweet, sweet, bacon candy. You can eat this on its own by the fistful, or use as a garnish to take your Bloody Marys to new, bacony heights. We've supplied three different flavours of glaze here so you have every excuse to make this over and over and over again.

MAKES 24

12 slices rindless streaky bacon, cut in half crossways

MAPLE PEPPER GLAZE

55 g (2 oz) dark brown sugar

60 ml (2 fl oz/¼ cup) pure maple syrup

2 teaspoons white-wine vinegar

1 teaspoon dijon mustard

freshly ground black pepper

ORANGE GLAZE

finely grated zest and juice of 1 orange

60 ml (2 fl oz/¼ cup) honey

STOUT GLAZE

110 g (4 oz/½ cup) soft brown sugar

60 ml (2 fl oz/¼ cup) stout or other dark beer

2 tablespoons pure maple syrup

Preheat the oven to 160°C/320°F (fan-forced). Line a large baking tray with foil and place a wire rack on top.

Mix all the ingredients of your glaze of choice together in a small bowl, until the mixture is syrupy.

Brush the bacon on both sides with the glaze and place in a single layer on the wire rack. Bake for 15 minutes. Remove from the oven and brush all over with more glaze. Return to the oven for a further 20-25 minutes, brushing with more glaze every 10 or so minutes, until the bacon is deeply browned and lacquered. Remove any pieces that are on the verge of burning. Keep a careful eye on it from about the 30-minute mark. It won't be totally crisp yet, but will crisp further on cooling.

Remove from the oven, cool on the rack for 5 minutes, and then transfer to a tray lined with a baking paper to cool completely.

Serve immediately, store in an airtight container in the fridge for 1-2 days or the freezer for up to 4 weeks. Refresh the bacon in an oven heated to 180°C (350°F) for 3-4 minutes if required.

NOTE: FOR BACON SPIRALS, USE LONG STRIPS OF BACON. AFTER THE FIRST 15 MINUTES OF BAKING AND WHEN YOU HAVE BRUSHED THE BACON WITH GLAZE FOR A SECOND TIME, TWIST THE BACON AROUND THE HANDLES OF WOODEN SPOONS AND CONTINUE TO BAKE UNTIL CRISP.

NOTE: FOR A SPICY KICK TO ANY OF THE GLAZES, ADD A SPLASH OF HOT SAUCE OR PINCH OF SMOKED HOT PAPRIKA, OR CAYENNE PEPPER.

Everything's better wrapped in bacon, and these tasty wedges are no exception. The avocado wedges may sound strange but they are a surprising, smooth yet crunchy treat.

SERVES 4-6

3 small (about 500 g/1 lb 2 oz) orange sweet potatoes, scrubbed well

17 slices rindless streaky bacon, halved lengthways

olive oil cooking spray

3 tablespoons plain (all-purpose) flour

1 large free-range egg, lightly beaten

60 g (2 oz/1 cup) panko (Japanese) breadcrumbs

3 tablespoons finely grated parmesan cheese

½ teaspoon ground coriander

½ teaspoon ground cumin

½ teaspoon sweet smoked paprika

2 firm ripe avocados, cut into 8 wedges each

salt flakes, to serve

SRIRACHA MAYO

150 g (5½ oz) good quality mayonnaise

about 1 tablespoon sriracha hot sauce

squeeze of lime juice, to taste

Preheat the oven to 200°C/400°F (fan-forced). Line two large baking trays with foil and place a wire rack on top of each.

Cut the sweet potato lengthways into wedges. You should get 6 wedges from each. Wrap each wedge with a bacon slice and place in a single layer over the prepared rack. Spray lightly with olive oil.

Bake for 10 minutes then move to a lower shelf in the oven. Increase the oven temperature to 210°C/410°F (fan-forced). Continue baking, for a further 15 minutes or until the potato is tender and the bacon is crisp.

Meanwhile, set up three shallow bowls in a row. Put the flour in the first bowl and season with salt and pepper. Place the egg into the middle bowl and combine the breadcrumbs, cheese, spices and a little more salt and pepper in the remaining bowl.

Working with one avocado wedge at a time, coat each wedge in the flour, shaking off the excess, followed by the beaten egg. Then roll in the breadcrumb mixture to coat well. Place on the second wire rack. Spray lightly with olive oil. Add to the top shelf of the oven, above the sweet potato, and bake for 13-15 minutes, until lightly browned and crisp.

Meanwhile for the sriracha mayo, combine the sriracha, mayonnaise and lime juice in a small bowl and set aside until required.

Sprinkle the wedges with salt flakes and serve on a platter with the sriracha mayo on the side for dipping.

Bacon-wrapped sweet potato with avocado wedges

These babies are totally moreish. Serve with some kind of delicious dipping sauce (think aioli or a smoky tomato sauce) for the perfect beer snack. They also make a great side dish for any meat, especially barbecue cooked low'n'slow.

Cheesy bacon & rosemary polenta chips

SERVES 4

250 g (9 oz) rindless loin (back) bacon, finely chopped

1 teaspoon finely chopped rosemary

1 litre (34 fl oz/4 cups) vegetable stock

210 g (7½ oz) instant (fine) polenta

100 g (3½ oz/1 cup) finely grated parmesan cheese

oil for deep-frying

finely chopped flat-leaf (Italian) parsley, to serve

salt flakes, to serve

Line a 33 cm x 23 cm (13 in x 9 in) baking tray with baking paper.

Cook the bacon in a large non-stick frying pan over medium heat for 6-8 minutes until browned and slightly crisp. Add the rosemary to the pan and stir for 1 minute. Transfer the bacon and rosemary to a plate.

Bring the stock to the boil in a large heavy-based saucepan over medium heat. Slowly whisk in the polenta. Stir for 2 minutes, or until thickened. Remove from the heat and stir in the bacon mixture and the cheese. Season with salt and pepper. Spoon the polenta into the prepared tray and set aside for 2-3 hours until set.

Turn out the polenta and trim the edges. Slice into strips 2 cm wide (you should get about 16) then cut each in half.

Heat the oil in a deep saucepan or deep-fryer to 190°C (375°F). A crumb added to the oil should sizzle immediately. Deep-fry the polenta chips, in small batches, for 2-3 minutes, until golden. Drain on paper towel.

Sprinkle with parsley and salt flakes to serve.

Bacon-wrapped sriracha onion rings

The holy trinity of savoury: bacon, sriracha and onion. These are a hit at parties (just make it a small party, you don't want to have to share) or serve in a pile with burgers or mac and cheese.

MAKES 8

4 large onions, peeled

3 tablespoons sriracha hot sauce

16 slices rindless streaky bacon, halved lengthways

125 g (4½ oz/ ½ cup) sour cream or Sriracha mayo (see page 18)

Line two large baking trays with foil and place a wire rack on top of each. (There's no need to pre-heat the oven for this recipe. It's better to start with a cold oven.)

Cut two 1.5 cm (½ in) wide rings from the widest part of each onion, being careful to keep the slices intact. Carefully pop out the centre two-thirds of each large ring, leaving two or three layers for each ring. You should have 8 onion rings. Save the leftover onion for another use.

Brush each onion ring with the hot sauce. Carefully wrap each coated ring with bacon, overlapping the bacon slightly as you wrap it around. You will need 4 strips of bacon for each ring. Secure the ends of the bacon strips with toothpicks as you go. Place the wrapped onion rings on the wire rack and place in the oven. Set the oven to 140°C/275°F (fan-forced) and bake for 30 minutes.

Increase the oven temperature to 160°C/320°F (fan-forced) and continue baking for a further 20-25 minutes until the onion is tender and the bacon is crisp.

Remove from the oven and carefully remove the toothpicks. Serve with the sour cream or sriracha mayo on the side for dipping.

These fritters contain broccoli so they're basically health food, right? Regardless of whether or not that's true, These are crazy good and make a great little snack, or even a perfectly bacony lunch if you serve them with a side salad.

Broccoli & bacon fritters with mustard sour cream

MAKES 8

1 large head broccoli, cut into florets

200 g (7 oz) rindless loin (back) bacon

50 g (1¾ oz/½ cup) grated parmesan cheese

75 g (2¾ oz/½ cup) plain (all-purpose) flour, sifted

¼ teaspoon baking powder

3 spring onions, finely chopped

2 large free-range eggs

80 ml (2½ fl oz ⅔ cup) sunflower, vegetable or rice bran oil

salt flakes, to serve

MUSTARD SOUR CREAM

300 g (10½ oz) sour cream

2 tablespoons lemon juice

1 teaspoon dijon mustard

Preheat the oven to 160°C/320°F (fan-forced). Line a baking tray with baking paper.

Lightly steam or microwave the broccoli for 2-3 minutes until just tender. Chop roughly.

Cook the bacon in a large non-stick frying pan over medium heat for 5 minutes or until lightly browned. Transfer to a chopping board to cool. Finely chop. Wipe out the pan.

Combine the broccoli and bacon in a large bowl. Add the cheese, flour, baking powder, spring onions and eggs. Season with salt and pepper and mix well.

Heat the oil in the frying pan and, once hot, add the batter in ⅓ cup amounts, not more than four at a time. Cook for 3-4 minutes on each side, or until golden. Transfer the fritters to the prepared baking tray and keep warm in the oven while you cook the rest.

For the mustard sour cream, combine the ingredients in a small bowl and season with salt and pepper.

Sprinkle the fritters with salt flakes and serve with the mustard sour cream on the side for dipping.

Cheesy puff-pastry * jalapeño & bacon twists

MAKES 12

2 sheets (about 350 g/12½ oz) butter puff pastry, just thawed

1 free-range egg, lightly beaten

90 g (3 oz/¾ cup) grated vintage cheddar cheese

25 g (1 oz/¼ cup) grated parmesan cheese

1 tablespoon roughly chopped pickled jalapeños

1 tablespoon dijon mustard

6 slices rindless streaky bacon, halved lengthways

sesame seeds, to sprinkle

Preheat the oven to 180°C/350°F (fan-forced). Line two large baking trays with baking paper.

Place one sheet of puff pastry on a chopping board. Brush with the egg and sprinkle with the cheeses and jalapeños. Brush the remaining sheet of pastry with egg and place egg-side down over the cheese-covered pastry. Press down on the pastry, firmly but gently, all over so it sticks together. Spread the top with the mustard and cut into 12 even strips. Gently separate one of the pastry strips, press a slice of bacon onto the top and twist. Place on the prepared baking tray, and then repeat with the remaining bacon and pastry. Brush each twist with a little more egg and sprinkle with sesame seeds.

Bake for 15 minutes until golden. Carefully turn the twists and bake for a further 5-8 minutes until the bacon is cooked through. Remove from the oven and cool slightly before diving in.

You can cool these twists on a wire rack and serve them at room temperature, but they're best eaten within an hour or two of baking.

These are ridiculously easy
to make so can be whipped
up immediately to sate any
bacon craving as it hits.
You can leave the jalapeños
out if you're a total chilli wimp,
but you might want to start
re-evaluating your life choices.

Break this out at a party
and the whole thing will
disappear in minutes, I promise
you. Or just prop yourself on
the couch with a whole bunch
of 80s action movies, this
dip and a big bag of corn chips
and you have yourself a
perfect Saturday night.

Cheesy bacon & mushroom dip

SERVES 8–10

1 tablespoon olive oil

20 g (¾ oz) butter

125 g (4½ oz) rindless loin (back) bacon, cut into thin strips

1 onion, finely sliced

200 g (7 oz) small portobello mushrooms, thinly sliced

2 garlic cloves, thinly sliced

125 g (4½ oz) cream cheese, softened

120 g (4½ oz/1 cup) grated Swiss cheese

60 g (2 oz/½ cup) grated vintage cheddar cheese

120 g (4½ oz/½ cup) light sour cream

2 spring onions, finely sliced, plus extra to serve

pinch of smoked hot paprika

sliced vegetables, crusty bread, corn chips or bagel chips, to serve

Preheat the oven to 160°C/320°F (fan-forced).

Heat the oil and butter in a large heavy-based frying pan over medium-high heat. Add the bacon and cook, stirring, for 6–8 minutes or until the bacon is crisp. Remove the bacon with a slotted spoon and drain on paper towel. Add the onion to the same pan, reduce the heat to medium and cook, stirring, for 3 minutes or until starting to soften. Add the mushrooms and garlic and cook, covered, stirring occasionally, for 5 minutes or until the mushrooms start to release their juices. Remove the lid, and cook, stirring occasionally, for 3–4 minutes or until the liquid has evaporated and the garlic is fragrant. Remove from the heat and set aside to cool for 5 minutes.

Add the cream cheese and stir until just combined, and then stir in the grated cheeses, sour cream, spring onions and half of the bacon. Spoon into a 700 ml (23½ fl oz) baking dish (or two 350 ml/12 fl oz dishes), sprinkle with the remaining bacon and the paprika and bake for 20–25 minutes or until the cheese mixture is heated through, melted and the top is golden.

Serve immediately with the accompaniments of your choice.

Bacon sides & salads

Bacon, beer & rosemary jam

MAKES ABOUT 2 ½ CUPS

500 g (1 lb 2 oz) rindless loin (back) bacon, chopped

2 tablespoons olive oil

2 onions, thinly sliced

2 garlic cloves, finely chopped

½ teaspoon chilli powder

1 sprig rosemary

150 g (5½ oz) soft brown sugar

375 ml (12½ fl oz/1½ cups) beer

160 ml (5½ fl oz/⅔ cup) malt vinegar

80 ml (2½ fl oz/⅓ cup) maple syrup

salt and freshly ground pepper

Put the bacon in a large, cold heavy-based frying pan over medium-high heat and cook, stirring occasionally, for 10 minutes or until well browned and crisp. Remove with a slotted spoon and drain on paper towel.

Add the oil and onions to the pan and cook over low heat for 10 minutes or until soft and caramelised. Add the garlic, chilli powder and rosemary and cook for 1 minute.

Return the bacon to the pan and then add the remaining ingredients and 500 ml (17 fl oz/2 cups) water. Simmer, uncovered, for 45-50 minutes until most of the liquid has reduced and the mixture is thick. Season to taste. Blend in a food processor until the bacon is finely chopped and the mixture is the consistency of a thick jam. Spoon into a large sterilised jar and store in the refrigerator.

NOTE: THIS JAM IS PARTICULARLY GOOD ON BURGERS AND SANDWICHES. IT HAS A LOVELY SALTY-SWEET PUNCH. IT IS BEST EATEN WITHIN 5 DAYS OF MAKING.

*THE THOUGHT OF NO BACON CAN MAKE A PERSON DO STRANGE THINGS. BUT DON'T LITERALLY BREAK THE GLASS - I'M SURE THERE'S A PERFECTLY GOOD LID ON THAT JAR.

Imagine you're making a sandwich or a burger and you open the fridge only to find that you've RUN out of bacon. It's a difficult and distressing thought to dwell on, so stay with me here just a moment longer. Imagine then, discovering that past-you had cooked up a batch of this jam: an in-case-of-emergency-break-glass* jar of bacon-laced jammy goodness to get you through the hard times.

Corn, bacon, kale & jalapeño salad

SERVES 4

4 slices middle (long-cut) bacon, rind removed

2 corn cobs, husks and silks removed

olive oil, for brushing

6–8 curly kale leaves, stems removed and leaves shredded

250 g (9 oz) mixed cherry tomatoes, halved

2 avocados, cut into thick slices

4 spring onions, finely chopped

½ jalapeño chilli, deseeded and thinly sliced

toasted pepitas (pumpkin seeds), to serve (optional)

TANGY LIME DRESSING

1 large egg yolk

80 ml (2½ fl oz/⅓ cup) lime juice

30 g (1 oz/1 cup) coriander (cilantro) leaves with some chopped stalk

2 teaspoons honey

½ jalapeño chilli, deseeded and thinly sliced

125 ml (4 fl oz/½ cup) olive oil

60 ml (2 fl oz/¼ cup) vegetable oil

If you absolutely must eat kale, the good news is that it goes brilliantly with bacon. Throw some corn and jalapeños in there and you'll barely even notice you're eating a salad.

Cook the bacon in a non-stick frying pan over medium-high heat for 6–8 minutes, turning occasionally until browned and crisp. Transfer to a chopping board and cut into pieces.

Meanwhile, preheat a barbecue grill to medium or a chargrill pan over medium heat.

Brush the corn with a little oil and cook on all sides until just charred and the kernels are tender. Remove, cool and cut off the kernels.

Combine the kale, tomato, avocado, corn, spring onion and chilli in a large salad bowl.

For the dressing, combine the egg yolk, lime juice, coriander, honey, chilli and a pinch of salt in a small food processor and blend until the coriander is finely chopped. Combine the oils in a jug. While the motor is running, pour in the oils in a slow steady stream until the mixture has thickened. Season with pepper. If the dressing is too thick, just add a small amount of warm water.

Lightly toss the salad ingredients with the dressing. Scatter the bacon pieces over and top with toasted pepitas, if using.

NOTE: YOU CAN SUBSTITUTE OTHER GREENS FOR THE KALE SUCH AS SHREDDED COS (ROMAINE) LETTUCE.

Asparagus wrapped in bacon

Because the best way to eat your greens is to wrap them in bacon. These actually make for a pretty classy side dish; they look fancy and work really well with any meat.

SERVES 4

2 bunches asparagus, ends trimmed

4 slices rindless streaky bacon

olive oil, to drizzle

1 tablespoon brown sugar

1 tablespoon toasted black sesame seeds

Preheat a barbecue grill to medium or a chargrill pan over medium heat.

Divide the asparagus into 4 bundles. Wrap each bundle with a slice of bacon and secure with a piece of kitchen string. Drizzle with a little olive oil.

Cook the asparagus, turning carefully every now and then, for 6-8 minutes or until the asparagus is lightly charred and the bacon is cooked through. Sprinkle all over with sugar and cook for a further 1-2 minutes until the sugar is caramelised.

Serve immediately scattered liberally with the sesame seeds and seasoned with pepper.

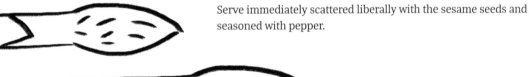

Cherry tomato & bacon skewers

These are amazingly simple to make yet they look properly sophisticated. Serve with anything you want to add a good punch of salt to, like grilled lamb chops or a nice juicy steak.

SERVES 4

250 g (9 oz) cherry tomatoes

250 g (9 oz) haloumi, cut into cubes

4 bamboo skewers, soaked in warm water for 30 minutes

4 slices rindless streaky bacon, cut in half lengthways

Preheat a barbecue grill to medium or a chargrill pan over medium heat.

Thread the cherry tomatoes and haloumi alternately onto the skewers, weaving the bacon on the skewer between the pieces. You will need two strips of bacon per skewer. If there is bacon left over at the end of each skewer, just keep threading it on.

Cook the skewers, turning carefully every now and then for 8–10 minutes until the haloumi is lightly charred and the bacon is cooked through. It's important not to have the barbecue or chargrill too hot as the bacon needs a chance to cook through before the tomatoes and cheese.

Season with a little salt and pepper to serve.

Braised cabbage with bacon

Do you know what goes really well with pork? Cabbage that's cooked with more pork. This is a classic accompaniment to pork chops, German-style sausages or pork knuckle. But don't feel that you have to be hemmed in here – this dish is also great with roast chicken or corned beef.

SERVES 4

1 tablespoon olive oil

40 g (1½ oz) butter

200 g (7 oz) rindless loin (back) bacon, cut into 1.5 cm (½ in) strips

1 onion, thinly sliced

½ small white cabbage, cored and shredded

80 ml (2½ fl oz/⅓ cup) dry white wine

1 teaspoon fennel seeds, lightly crushed

2 tablespoons chopped flat-leaf (Italian) parsley

Heat the oil and butter in a large heavy-based saucepan over medium heat. Add the bacon and cook, stirring, for 4-5 minutes until well browned and crisp around the edges. Remove with a slotted spoon and set aside.

Add the onion to the pan and cook, stirring, for 2-3 minutes until lightly browned. Add the cabbage, then pour in the wine and season well. Cover, reduce the heat slightly and cook gently for 10-12 minutes, stirring occasionally, or until the cabbage is tender. Return the bacon to the pan, add the fennel seeds and cook, uncovered, for a further couple of minutes or until heated through. Stir in the parsley, season and serve immediately.

Bacon, broad beans & ricotta

This delicious combo is great with eggs or any kind of roast. You can also toss it through cooked pasta with some extra-virgin olive oil. Add finely chopped chilli or chilli flakes to give it a nice kick.

SERVES 4

500 g (1 lb 2 oz) shelled broad (fava) beans

280 g (10 oz) rindless loin (back) bacon, chopped

2 garlic cloves, finely chopped

120 g (4½ oz/½ cup) fresh ricotta

small handful mint leaves, torn

lemon cheeks, for squeezing

Bring a saucepan of water to the boil. Add the broad beans, bring back to the boil and cook for 3-5 minutes, until just tender. Drain the beans and peel and discard the skins. Set aside.

Cook the bacon in a large non-stick frying pan over medium heat for 8 minutes, or until browned and slightly crisp. Add the garlic and broad beans and cook, stirring, for 1-2 minutes until everything is combined and the garlic is fragrant. Season with salt and pepper.

Spoon the mixture into a serving bowl. Crumble the ricotta over the top and sprinkle with the mint. Serve with lemon cheeks on the side.

Creamy bacon scalloped potatoes

Layers of potato cooked slowly in cream and cheese ... Classic scalloped potato is just begging for a bit of bacon. Use a wide, shallow dish to cook this in to maximise the amount of crunchy cheesy top (which we all know is the best bit).

SERVES 4

1 tablespoon olive oil

20 g (¾ oz) butter

200 g (7 oz) rindless loin (back) bacon, cut into strips

1 leek, pale part only, thinly sliced

1 kg (2 lb 3 oz) potatoes, very thinly sliced using a mandoline or food processor

2 garlic cloves, thinly sliced

400 ml (13½ fl oz) thickened (whipping) cream (35% fat)

25 g (1 oz/¼ cup) grated parmesan cheese

1 spring onion, finely sliced

Preheat the oven to 160°C/320°F (fan-forced). Lightly grease a large roasting pan or baking dish.

Heat the oil and butter in a large heavy-based lidded frying pan over medium heat. Add the bacon and cook, stirring, for 6-8 minutes until crisp. Remove with a slotted spoon and drain on paper towel. Set aside.

Add the leek to the same pan and cook, stirring, for 4-5 minutes until tender. Add the potato, garlic and cream, season well and bring to the boil, stirring gently. Cover and simmer for 8-10 minutes until the potato is just starting to soften.

Remove from the heat and carefully spoon into the prepared pan. Scatter with the bacon, poking it between the potato slices in a few places. Sprinkle with the cheese.

Bake for 25-30 minutes until tender and golden. If the top begins to brown too much, cover with foil. Remove from the oven and rest for 5 minutes. Serve scattered with the spring onion.

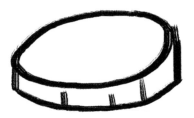

Bacon Mains

Breakfast salad

This is everything that's great about a classic fry-up breakfast, in salad form. If you're a quitter who can't be bothered making the potato nuggets, a bag of shop-bought tater tots will also do.

SERVES 4

4 large very fresh free-range eggs

2 teaspoons white vinegar

4 slices bacon

2 baby cos (romaine) lettuces, leaves separated

1 avocado, sliced

fresh herbs, to serve

POTATO NUGGETS

500 g (1 lb 2 oz) waxy potatoes (such as desiree), unpeeled and cut into quarters

½ small onion, grated

1 teaspoon plain (all-purpose) flour

¼ teaspoon salt

peanut oil for deep-frying

HOLLANDAISE SAUCE

3 egg yolks

1 tablespoon lemon juice

60 g (2 oz) butter, cut into 1.5 cm (½ in) cubes, softened

2 teaspoons chopped herbs

2 teaspoons capers, rinsed and chopped

TIP: JUST BECAUSE THIS DISH HAS THE WORD 'BREAKFAST IN THE TITLE, THERE'S NO REASON TO TAKE THAT AS GOSPEL: THIS MAKES A FANTASTIC LUNCH OR KILLER DINNER.

For the potato nuggets, put the potatoes in a large saucepan and cover with water. Bring to the boil and simmer for 8-10 minutes or until barely tender. Drain and allow to cool to the point you can handle them, then peel and coarsely grate. The potato should be quite sticky. Place in a large bowl along with the onion, flour and salt. Season with pepper and mix gently with a fork.

Preheat the oven to 140°C/275°F (fan-forced). Line a large baking tray with baking paper. Heat the oil in a deep saucepan or deep-fryer to 180°C (350°F). A crumb added to the oil should sizzle immediately. Shape heaped teaspoons of the potato mixture gently into oval shapes. Fry in batches of 4-5 at a time for 3-4 minutes until golden brown. Drain on paper towel and keep warm in the oven on the prepared tray.

Meanwhile, for the hollandaise sauce, whisk the egg yolks and lemon juice in a large heatproof bowl. Place the bowl over a saucepan of simmering water over low heat. The bowl should fit snugly over the top of the saucepan with the bottom not touching the water. Whisk for 3 minutes or until the mixture becomes thick and pale. Add the butter one cube at a time, whisking until melted before adding the next. This may take 6-8 minutes. Remove from the heat. Stir in the herbs and capers and season with salt and pepper. Set aside in a warm spot, covered, whisking occasionally until ready to serve. It should hold for 30 or so minutes.If required, thin the hollandaise by whisking in a little warm water just before serving.

Put the bacon in a large, cold heavy-based frying pan and place over medium-high heat. Cook for about 3 minutes on each side.

Meanwhile, fill a deep frying pan with boiling water from the kettle. Bring to a light simmer over medium heat and add the vinegar. Crack one of the eggs into a cup and gently pour it into the water in one fluid movement. Repeat with the remaining eggs. Cook for 3-4 minutes, until the whites are set, but the yolk still runny.

Divide the lettuce between four large serving bowls. Top with the avocado, bacon, poached eggs and potato nuggets. Drizzle with the hollandaise and sprinkle with herbs. Serve immediately.

Bacon Hash

This really is the ultimate hangover breakfast, lunch or dinner. Packed with carbs and salt, it's good for what ails you and it's already in bite-sized pieces for ease of recovery. All you need is someone else to cook it for you...

SERVES 4

1 kg (2 lb 3 oz) waxy potatoes (such as desiree), cut into 2 cm (¾ in) dice

280 g (10 oz) rindless loin (back) bacon, chopped

60 ml (2 fl oz/¼ cup) olive oil

1 red capsicum, finely chopped

2 garlic cloves, crushed

1 teaspoon smoked paprika

2 sprigs thyme

4 spring onions, finely chopped

4 free-range eggs

Place the potato in a large saucepan and cover with cold water. Bring to the boil and cook the potatoes for 2 minutes, or until just tender. Drain well.

Cook the bacon in a large non-stick frying pan over medium-high heat for 8-10 minutes, until very crisp. Using a slotted spoon, transfer the bacon to a plate. Add the potatoes to the pan and cook for 10 minutes over medium heat, until browned and crisp. Transfer to the plate with the bacon.

Add 2 tablespoons of the oil and the capsicum to the pan and cook for 2-3 minutes until the capsicum has softened. Stir in the garlic, paprika and thyme and cook for 1 minute. Return the bacon and potatoes to the pan and toss until warmed through. Season well with salt and pepper. Stir in the spring onion then transfer the mixture to a serving plate or plates.

Meanwhile, heat the remaining oil in a frying pan over medium-high heat and fry the eggs until cooked to your liking. Serve on top of the hash.

Slow-cooked bacon & beans

Rich, sweet and smoky, these are everything you ever wanted baked beans to be but never were - you'll never even look at the tinned stuff again. Fantastic with eggs or with big slabs of buttery sourdough for dipping.

SERVES 4

250 g (9 oz) dried white beans (such as cannellini/lima beans)

280 g (10 oz) rindless loin (back) bacon, chopped

1 onion, finely chopped

1 garlic clove, finely chopped

½ teaspoon smoked paprika

70 g (2½ oz/¼ cup) tomato paste

55 g (2 oz/¼ cup) soft brown sugar

2 tablespoons molasses

2 teaspoons Worcestershire sauce

1 litre (34 fl oz/4 cups) vegetable stock

toasted sourdough, to serve

soft goat's cheese, to serve (optional)

flat-leaf (Italian) parsley leaves, roughly chopped, to serve

Soak the beans in cold water for 6-8 hours or overnight. Drain.

Cook the bacon in a large (preferably non-stick) saucepan over medium heat for 6-8 minutes, until browned. Add the onion and cook for 10 minutes over low heat, until soft. Add the garlic and paprika and cook for 1 minute until fragrant. Stir in the tomato paste, sugar, molasses, Worcestershire sauce and stock. Increase the heat, cover and bring to the boil. Reduce the heat to low again and simmer for 1 hour 45 minutes, stirring occasionally.

Remove the lid and simmer for a further 15 minutes, or until the beans are tender and the sauce thickened.

Spread the toasted sourdough with goat's cheese, if desired. Serve the beans alongside the sourdough with parsley sprinkled over the top.

Bacon & egg lasagne

SERVES 6

300 g (10½ oz) rindless loin (back) bacon, cut into 1.5 cm (½ in) strips

1 leek, pale part only, thinly sliced

3 garlic cloves, crushed

1 tablespoon chopped herbs (such as thyme, oregano, parsley), plus extra to garnish

375 g (13 oz) fresh lasagne sheets

200 g (7 oz) bocconcini, sliced

9 large free-range eggs

75 g (2¾ oz/¾ cups) grated parmesan

CHEESY BÉCHAMEL SAUCE

1 small onion

6 cloves

750 ml (25½ fl oz/3 cups) full-cream (whole) milk

1 bay leaf

50 g (1¾ oz) unsalted butter

50 g (1¾ oz/⅓ cup) plain (all-purpose) flour

75 g (2¾ oz/¾ cups) grated parmesan

Preheat the oven to 160°C/320°F (fan-forced). Lightly grease a 2 litre (68 fl oz/8 cup) baking dish. To make the béchamel sauce, stud the onion with the cloves, then place in a saucepan with the milk and the bay leaf. Bring the milk just to the boil over medium heat then set aside to infuse for 10 minutes. Strain into a jug, discarding the onion and bay leaf. Melt the butter in a clean saucepan over a medium-low heat. Stir in the flour and cook, stirring, for 2-3 minutes until the mixture bubbles and dries out slightly. Add the milk gradually, whisking until the sauce comes to the boil and is thick and smooth. Remove from the heat. Season well with salt and pepper, stir in the parmesan and mix until combined. Cover the surface with some plastic wrap or baking paper to prevent a skin from forming and set aside until needed.

Meanwhile, put the bacon in a large, cold heavy-based frying pan and cook, stirring, over medium-high heat for 6-8 minutes until crisp. Remove with a slotted spoon and drain on paper towel. Add the leek and garlic to the pan, reduce the heat and cook, stirring, for 4-5 minutes until tender. Remove from the heat, return the bacon to the pan, stir in the herbs and set aside.

Spread a spoonful of the cheesy sauce over the base of the prepared baking dish. Top with one layer of the lasagne sheets, then one-quarter of the remaining sauce. Make three indents in the cheese sauce and crack in three of the eggs. Sprinkle with one-third each of the bacon mixture and bocconcini, then repeat twice. Finish with a layer of lasagne sheets and the remaining cheese sauce and the parmesan. Bake for 35-40 minutes until the pasta is tender and the top is golden brown. Allow to rest for 10 minutes before serving. Garnish with fresh herbs.

'Breakfast', 'lunch', 'dinner' – why do we have to have so many labels for things? This lasagne laughs in the face of outmoded ideas of categorisation and is equally awesome eaten at any time of day or night.

Bacon-weave BLT

The perfect **BLT** with just the right amount of bacon in every bite! Alternatively, you can ditch the bread, make two bacon weaves and sandwich the ingredients in between for a **BLT** bacon bonanza.

SERVES I

4 slices rindless streaky bacon, cut in half lengthways

1 slice Swiss cheese (optional)

2 square slices bread of your choice

mayonnaise, to spread

lettuce leaves, trimmed to fit the bread

½ avocado, sliced or mashed

4 thin slices tomato

Preheat the oven to 180°C/350°F (fan-forced). Line a baking tray with foil, folding up the edges of the foil to contain the rendered bacon fat.

Make a weave or lattice with the bacon strips following the instructions on page 10, to form a square on the prepared tray. Place an upturned wire rack over the bacon to keep it flat while it cooks. Cook the bacon for 25-30 minutes until browned and crisp. Remove from the oven, carefully remove the rack and place the bacon weave on paper towel. You may like to trim it with sharp scissors to fit the size of the bread slices. If using the cheese, lay it on top of the bacon to warm.

Spread the bread with mayonnaise. Top with lettuce, avocado and tomato, season with salt and pepper, then top with the bacon weave and the other slice of bread. Serve immediately.

Bacon-weave cheeseburgers

SERVES 4

600 g (1 lb 5 oz) minced (ground) beef

2 onions, 1 grated, 1 thinly sliced

1 teaspoon dijon mustard

1 large free-range egg, beaten

40 g (1½ oz/½ cup) fresh breadcrumbs

35 g (1¼ oz/⅓ cup) finely grated parmesan cheese

12 slices rindless streaky bacon

4 soft burger buns, split horizontally

4 slices Swiss cheese

1 red onion, thinly sliced

mayonnaise, sliced dill pickles, shredded lettuce and thinly sliced tomato, to serve

Preheat the oven to 180°C/350°F (fan-forced). Line a baking tray with foil, folding up the edges of the foil to contain the rendered bacon fat. Combine the beef, grated onion, mustard, egg, breadcrumbs and parmesan in a bowl. Season, mix with damp hands, and then form into 4 patties. Chill for 30 minutes.

Meanwhile, make a weave or lattice with the bacon strips following the instructions on page 10, to form a square on the prepared tray. Place an upturned wire rack over the bacon to keep it flat while it cooks. Cook the bacon for 25–30 minutes until browned and crisp. Remove from the oven, carefully remove the rack and place the bacon weave on paper towel. Cut into four even squares. Drain all the rendered fat from the bacon tray into a large heavy-based (preferably cast iron) frying pan. Turn off the oven and place the bacon weave on the tray. Keep warm in the oven.

Brush the cut side of each of the buns with the bacon fat. Set aside. Heat the frying pan with the remaining bacon fat over medium-high heat. Put the patties in the hot pan, flatten slightly and cook for 8–10 minutes until well crusted and browned, turning occasionally. Top the patties with the cheese slices and cook for a minute or so more until the cheese starts to melt and the patties are just cooked through. Transfer to a plate.

Add the sliced onion to the pan and cook, stirring often, for 4–5 minutes until tender and browned. Pile on top of the cheese on the patties. Meanwhile, grill the cut side of the burger buns until golden. Spread mayonnaise on the toasted side of each bun. Place a few slices of pickle on each bottom bun. Top with lettuce, tomato, a patty and a square of bacon weave. Close the buns and serve.

Salty bacon is the perfect foil for a big juicy beef burger slathered in cheese. The bacon weave really brings this to a whole new level of burger perfection.

Mac & Cheese in a burger?
Why the hell not. We might as
well wrap it in bacon while we're here.
Try making the patties on
their own for a fantastic snack
(Obviously, you'll need to add
some chopped fried bacon though).

Bacon-wrapped mac & cheese burgers

MAKES 6

250 g (9 oz) macaroni

40 g (1½ oz) butter

2 shallots, finely chopped

1½ tablespoons plain (all-purpose) flour, plus extra for coating

250 ml (8½ fl oz/1 cup) full-cream (whole) milk

125 g (4½ oz/1 cup) grated Gruyere or smoked cheddar cheese

75 g (2¾ oz/¾ cup) finely grated parmesan cheese

2 large free-range eggs, lightly beaten

80 g (2¾ oz/1⅓ cups) panko (Japanese) breadcrumbs

125 ml (4 fl oz/½ cup) sunflower or vegetable oil

6 slices middle (long-cut) bacon (about 40 cm/16 in), rind removed

6 rolls or brioche buns, halved and toasted

dijonnaise, good quality aioli or smoky tomato sauce, to serve

lettuce and sliced tomato, to serve

Line a 33 cm x 23 cm (13 in x 9 in) baking tray with baking paper. Bring a large saucepan of salted water to the boil. Cook the macaroni according to the packet directions or until al dente, stirring often to prevent sticking. Drain.

Meanwhile, melt the butter in a saucepan. Add the shallots and cook for 3–4 minutes until soft. Stir in the flour. Remove from the heat and slowly stir in the milk. Return to the heat and gently bring to the boil, stirring until thickened. Remove from the heat and stir in the cheeses until melted. Season with salt and pepper then stir in the macaroni until well combined. Pour into the prepared tray, pressing down with a wooden spoon to compact the macaroni mixture. Refrigerate for at least 3 hours to set.

Turn the macaroni out onto a clean work surface and cut into six rounds using a 9 cm (3½ in) cutter. (Save any leftover mac and cheese and reheat as a snack.)

Place the extra flour, egg and breadcrumbs into three separate shallow bowls. Coat each macaroni patty in the flour, shaking off the excess, followed by the beaten egg, then into the breadcrumbs, pressing on to coat well. Place onto a plate.

Heat the oil in a large non-stick frying pan until very hot. Shallow-fry the patties, three at a time, for 2–3 minutes on each side until golden. Transfer to a plate lined with paper towel to drain. Discard the oil and wipe out the pan. Wrap a rasher of bacon the whole way around each patty and secure the ends with a toothpick. Heat the pan. Cook the bacon-wrapped patties, three at a time, for 3–4 minutes on each side, or until the bacon is golden. Remove the toothpicks. Serve on the toasted buns spread with dijonnaise, topped with lettuce and tomato.

Bacon-wrapped garlic & herb chicken drumsticks

Not only does the bacon-wrapping here add a delicious bacon layer to a previously bacon-free foodstuff, but it also helps keep moisture in, resulting in super tender and juicy drumsticks.

SERVES 4

8 chicken drumsticks

2 teaspoons olive oil

8 slices middle (long-cut) bacon, rind removed

salad, to serve (optional)

GARLIC & HERB BUTTER

80 g (2¾ oz) butter, softened

1 garlic clove, crushed

2 teaspoons chopped parsley

Preheat the oven to 160°C/320°F (fan-forced). Line a roasting pan with baking paper.

Toss the chicken in the oil. Heat a large non-stick frying pan over medium-high heat and cook the chicken for 10–12 minutes, turning often, until well browned all over. Remove from the heat and transfer to a plate to cool slightly.

Meanwhile, for the garlic and herb butter, combine the ingredients in a small bowl. Mix well.

Spread one side of each of the bacon slices with a little of the garlic butter. When the chicken is cool enough to handle, wrap a slice of bacon around each drumstick, with the buttery side against the chicken skin. Secure with kitchen string or toothpicks, if necessary, and place in the prepared pan.

Roast for 35–40 minutes, basting with the pan juices after 20 minutes, until the bacon is well browned and the chicken cooked through. Serve drizzled with the delicious pan juices, with salad on the side, if desired.

Meat wrapped in bacon, what could possibly be better? Proudly cloaked in its bacon weave, this is a seriously pimped take on the humble meatloaf.

Bacon-wrapped meatloaf

SERVES 4

1 tablespoon olive oil

1 onion, finely chopped

2 medium-sized carrots, coarsely grated

2 garlic cloves, crushed

400 g (14 oz) minced (ground) pork

400 g (14 oz) minced (ground) veal

45 g (¾ cup) fresh breadcrumbs

50 g (1¾ oz/½ cup) finely grated parmesan cheese

1 tablespoon chopped sage

1 tablespoon chopped flat-leaf (Italian) parsley

½ teaspoon salt

60 ml (2 fl oz/¼ cup) barbecue sauce, plus 1 tablespoon extra, to glaze

1 large free-range egg

1 teaspoon dijon mustard

6 slices rindless streaky bacon

Preheat the oven to 180°C/350°F (fan-forced).

Heat the oil in a large heavy-based frying pan over low heat and cook the onion for 5 minutes or until soft. Add the carrot and garlic and cook for a further minute or until fragrant. Transfer to a large bowl and set aside to cool.

Add the meat, breadcrumbs, cheese, herbs, salt, barbecue sauce, egg and mustard to the bowl. Mix well. Form into a log shape and place on a wire rack set over a roasting pan.

Make a weave or lattice with the bacon strips following the instructions on page 10, to form a square. Lay the weave over the top of the meatloaf, tucking the edges of the bacon underneath. Brush with the extra barbecue sauce. Bake for 15 minutes then reduce the oven to 160°C/320°F (fan-forced) and cook a further 25-30 minutes, or until the meatloaf is firm and cooked through.

Allow to rest for 10 minutes before serving.

How do you make the ultimate comfort food a thousand million times better than it already is? Clearly everything tastes better with bacon, so this is a serious no-brainer. Also, this recipe uses cream instead of a béchamel sauce, so it's ultra simple to make.

SERVES 4

250 g (9 oz) macaroni

500 ml (17 fl oz/2 cups) thickened (whipping) cream (35% fat)

1 large garlic clove, smashed

1 large sprig thyme

200 g (7 oz) rindless loin (back) bacon, chopped

180 g (6½ oz/1½ cups) grated cheddar cheese

100 g (3½ oz/1 cup) finely grated parmesan cheese

pinch of freshly grated nutmeg

70 g (2½ oz/1 cup) fresh breadcrumbs

2 tablespoons olive oil

pinch of smoked paprika

Bring a large saucepan of salted water to the boil. Cook the macaroni according to packet directions, or until al dente. Drain.

Meanwhile, preheat the oven to 180°C/350°F (fan-forced). Lightly grease a 22 cm (8¾ in) square 1 litre (34 fl oz/4 cup) baking dish.

Combine the cream, garlic and thyme in a saucepan over medium heat. Bring to a simmer, then remove from the heat and allow to infuse for a few minutes.

Cook the bacon in a non-stick frying pan over medium-high heat for 6–8 minutes until slightly browned and crisp.

Strain the solids from the cream mixture. Strip the thyme leaves and return to the cream, discarding the stem. Add 1 cup of the cheddar cheese and all of the parmesan and nutmeg and stir until the cheeses have melted. Season with salt and pepper. Add the macaroni and bacon to the cream mixture and stir until well coated. Pour into the prepared dish.

Combine the breadcrumbs, remaining cheddar cheese and the oil in a bowl and sprinkle over the top of the macaroni mixture. Sprinkle with a little smoked paprika. Bake for 10 minutes until golden and crunchy.

Oozy bacon
mac & cheese

Smoky pork
& bacon
tacos

SERVES 4-6

1 tablespoon olive oil

1 kg (2 lb 3 oz) piece pork scotch fillet (pork neck), skin removed, or boneless pork shoulder (butt)

1 teaspoon ground cumin

1 teaspoon hot smoked paprika

1 onion, chopped

4 garlic cloves, crushed

125 ml (4 fl oz/½ cup) tomato passata (puréed tomatoes)

2 tablespoons Worcestershire sauce

1 tablespoon molasses

½ teaspoon good quality liquid smoke (optional)

large handful coriander (cilantro) leaves

12 corn tortillas, warmed

lime wedges, to serve

BACON & TOMATO SALSA

200 g (7 oz) rindless loin (back) bacon, cut into 1.5 cm (½ in) strips

2 tomatoes, chopped

2 spring onions, finely sliced

50 g (1¾ oz) feta cheese, crumbled

juice of ½ lime

These tacos pack a big, zingy flavour punch. You could aslo just make the bacon and tomato salsa and serve it as a dip or use it as a delicious topping for nachos.

Preheat the oven to 140°C/275°F (fan-forced).

Heat the oil in a small heavy-based casserole or Dutch oven over medium-high heat. Coat the pork in the cumin and paprika. Cook for 6-7 minutes, turning, until browned all over. Transfer to a plate. Reduce the heat and add the onion and garlic. Cook, stirring, for 5 minutes or until lightly browned. Add the passata, Worcestershire sauce, molasses, liquid smoke (if using) and 60 ml (2 fl oz/¼ cup) water and bring to the boil.

Remove from the heat, return the pork to the casserole, cover with a tight-fitting lid and bake for 1½ hours or until tender. Remove the lid and cook for a further 30 minutes or until the pork is very tender and pulls apart easily with two forks. Remove from the oven and set aside to rest for 15 minutes.

To make the bacon and tomato salsa, at about the time the pork is removed from the oven, put the bacon in a large heavy-based frying pan over medium-high heat. Cook, stirring occasionally, for 6-8 minutes until browned and crisp around the edges. Drain on paper towel, then transfer to a large bowl. Add the tomato, spring onion and feta. Squeeze over a little lime juice and toss gently to combine.

Shred, or 'pull', the pork with two forks, discarding any fatty bits. Return to the casserole and stir to combine with the sauce. Toss in the coriander. Serve the warmed tortillas topped with the pulled pork, bacon salsa, with lime wedges for squeezing.

The ultimate bacony pasta carbonara

A well-made carbonara is the ultimate crowd-pleaser. It can be thrown together quickly for a simple sunday night dinner on the couch, yet works just as well as a classy dish to pull out when you really want to impress someone special.

SERVES 4

400 g (14 oz) spaghetti

250 g (9 oz) rindless loin (back) bacon, chopped

1 large garlic clove, finely chopped

4 egg yolks

125 ml (4 fl oz/½ cup) thickened (whipping) cream (35% fat)

75 g (2¾ oz/¾ cup) finely grated parmesan cheese, plus extra to serve

1 tablespoon chopped flat-leaf (Italian) parsley

Bring a large saucepan of salted water to the boil. Cook the spaghetti according to the packet directions or until al dente, stirring often to prevent sticking. Drain, reserving some of the cooking water.

Meanwhile, cook the bacon in a large non-stick frying pan over medium–high heat for 6–8 minutes until browned and slightly crisp. Add the garlic and cook a further minute or until fragrant.

Combine the egg yolks, cream and parmesan in a medium-sized bowl. Season with salt and pepper.

Return the spaghetti to the saucepan with a tablespoon or two of the cooking water. Add the bacon and garlic to the pan. Mix the egg mixture through until well coated and creamy. Stir in the parsley.

Serve with extra parmesan cheese sprinkled over the top.

Bacon Drinks and Desserts

The ultimate breakfast cocktail made even more breakfast-ready with the addition of bacon-infused vodka.
The vodka takes up to a week to make so you'll need to plan ahead for this one.

SERVES 1

90 ml (3 fl oz) tomato juice

30–60 ml (2–3 fl oz)
Bacon-infused vodka (see below)

splash lemon or lime juice

½ teaspoon dijon mustard

dash of Worcestershire sauce

dash of hot sauce
(sriracha or Tabasco)

1 long slice cucumber

1 piece Candied bacon with
maple pepper glaze
(see page 17)

1 cherry tomato

1 sprig coriander (cilantro)

MAKES ABOUT 750 ML (25½ FL OZ/3 CUPS)

6 pieces Candied bacon
with maple pepper glaze
(see page 17), roughly chopped

750 ml (25½ fl oz/3 cups) vodka

Fill a cocktail shaker with ice and add the tomato juice, vodka, lemon or lime juice, mustard and sauces and season generously with salt and pepper. Seal and shake vigorously but briefly, then strain into a tall glass half-filled with more ice. Garnish with the cucumber, candied bacon, tomato and coriander. Serve immediately.

- - - - - - - - - - - - - - -

Bacon-infused vodka

Sterilise an 800 ml (27 fl oz) jar and lid. Add the bacon and pour in the vodka, keeping the bottle for later use. Close the jar, give it a bit of a shake and then refrigerate for 3–7 days until the flavour has infused to your liking.

Line a sieve with a coffee filter or double layer of muslin (cheese cloth) and strain the vodka into a jug. Repeat the process if there are any specs of fat remaining in the vodka. Carefully pour the infused vodka back into the reserved bottle. Discard the bacon. Store in the refrigerator.

- - - - - - - - - - - - - - -

Spicy bacon Bloody Mary

This is like the best Cuba Libre ever, combined with the classic childhood ice cream soda.
Plus bacon! We may have invented the ultimate drink here ...

Bacon-bourbon ice cream soda

Put a few of cubes of ice in a tall glass and pour in the bourbon. Fill the glass to about two-thirds full with the cola. Add the scoop of ice cream and serve immediately with a long spoon and a straw.

SERVES 1

30 ml (1 fl oz) Bacon-infused bourbon (see below)

250 ml (8½ fl oz/1 cup) chilled cola

1 scoop Bacon and pecan brittle ice cream (see page 80) or vanilla ice cream

MAKES ABOUT 750 ML (25½ FL OZ/ 3 CUPS)

6 pieces Candied bacon with orange glaze (see page 17), roughly chopped

750 ml (25½ fl oz/3 cups) bourbon

Bacon-infused bourbon

Sterilise an 800 ml (27 fl oz) jar and lid. Add the bacon and pour in the bourbon, keeping the bottle for later use. Close the jar, give it a bit of a shake and then refrigerate for 3-7 days until the flavour has infused to your liking.

Line a sieve with a coffee filter or double layer of muslin (cheese cloth) and strain the bourbon into a jug. Repeat the process if there are any specs of fat remaining in the bourbon. Carefully pour the infused bourbon back into the reserved bottle. Discard the bacon. Store in the refrigerator.

Vanilla bacon monster shake

This is the last word in over-the-top ridiculousness – when too much sweet and salty bacon just isn't enough, it's time for a monster shake. Bring it on, I say.

SERVES 1 (OR 2 IF YOU WANT TO SHARE)

50 g (1¾ oz) dark chocolate, melted

2 scoops Bacon and pecan brittle ice cream (page 80) or vanilla ice cream

400 ml (13½ fl oz) chilled full-cream (whole) milk

canned whipped cream, to serve

1 Bacon donut (page 86)

Honey caramel, bacon and macadamia popcorn, to serve (page 14)

1 piece Dark chocolate-covered candied bacon with sprinkles (page 84)

Drizzle the melted chocolate around the inside of a mason jar or tall glass. Set aside.

Put the ice cream and milk in a blender or milkshake maker and blend until combined and frothy. Pour into the prepared jar or glass. Top with whipped cream, the donut, more whipped cream, a sprinkling of popcorn and the candied bacon. Serve immediately.

NOTE: YOU CAN WHIP YOUR OWN CREAM FOR THIS RECIPE IF YOU REALLY WANT – WHISK SOME THICKENED (WHIPPING) CREAM WITH A LITTLE ADDED ICING (CONFECTIONERS') SUGAR TO MEDIUM-FIRM PEAKS AND SPOON INTO A PIPING BAG FITTED WITH A STAR NOZZLE.

Bacon & pecan brittle ice cream

MAKES ABOUT 1 LITRE (34 FL OZ/ 4 CUPS)

150 g (5½ oz) rindless bacon, roughly chopped

500 ml (17 fl oz/2 cups) full-cream (whole) milk

250 ml (8½ fl oz/1 cup) thickened (whipping) cream (35% fat)

1 teaspoon vanilla bean paste

2 tablespoons Bacon-infused bourbon (see page 77) (optional)

5 extra-large free-range egg yolks

150 g (5½ oz/⅔ cup, firmly packed) brown sugar

Put the bacon in a large, cold heavy-based frying pan and cook, stirring occasionally, over medium-high heat for 6-8 minutes until well browned. Remove with a slotted spoon and drain on paper towel.

Put the cooked bacon in a large jug or bowl and add the milk. Mix well. Cover and refrigerate overnight for the flavours to infuse.

The next day, pour the milk and bacon into a medium heavy-based saucepan and add the cream and vanilla paste. Cook, stirring constantly, over medium-low heat until the mixture just comes to the boil. Stir in the bourbon (if using). Remove from the heat and set aside.

Whisk the egg yolks and sugar in a large bowl until thickened. Gradually whisk in the warm milk mixture, and then pour back into the saucepan. Return the pan to a medium heat and cook, stirring constantly until the mixture thickens slightly and coats the back of a spoon (85°C/185°F on a sugar thermometer).

Strain the ice cream custard mixture into a large bowl set over an ice bath, discarding the solids, and stir until cold. Cover and refrigerate the custard for at least 4 hours until thoroughly chilled, preferably overnight.

You'll need to start this ice cream two days ahead, to allow for all of the bacony goodness to infuse. But it is well worth the wait, I assure you.

BACON & PECAN BRITTLE

100 g (3½ oz) rindless bacon, cut into 1 cm (½ in) dice

75 g (2¾ oz/⅓ cup) caster (superfine) sugar

1 tablespoon glucose syrup

40 g (1½ oz) butter, chopped

¼ teaspoon bicarbonate of soda (baking soda)

35 g (¼ oz/¼ cup) pecans, roughly chopped

Meanwhile, to make the bacon and pecan brittle, line a large baking tray with non-stick baking paper. Put the bacon in a large, cold heavy-based frying pan over medium–high heat and cook, stirring occasionally, for 6–8 minutes until well browned. Remove with a slotted spoon and drain on paper towel. Put the sugar, glucose syrup and 3 tablespoons water in a saucepan over medium heat. Cook, gently swirling occasionally, until the glucose has dissolved. Bring to the boil and cook, without stirring, until the caramel is golden, about 5 minutes. Remove from the heat and add the butter gradually, whisking until combined. Stir in the bicarbonate of soda, being careful as the mixture will bubble up slightly. Working quickly, stir in the pecans and pour the mixture onto the prepared tray. Set aside for at least 30 minutes to set and cool. Roughly chop the brittle into bite-sized pieces.

Churn the prepared custard in an ice cream machine according to the manufacturer's instructions. Working quickly, scoop the ice cream into a chilled 1.25 litre (42 fl oz/5 cup) container, alternating with sprinkles of the brittle (reserve some of the brittle to spinkle on top). Gently swirl to ripple through the mixture and finally scatter with the remaining brittle. Freeze for 1½–2 hours to firm up before serving.

Dark chocolate-covered candied bacon with sprinkles

Choose your favourite candied bacon flavour for this recipe; they all work well. Wrap these in cellophane bags tied with ribbon for a gift that will put a smile on anyone's face (and make them worship you as the god of bacon that you are).

MAKES 12

150 g (5½ oz) dark chocolate, chopped

12 slices Candied bacon (page 17)

sprinkles, to coat

Line a large baking tray with baking paper.

Melt two-thirds of the chocolate gently in a small heatproof bowl set over a pan of simmering water. Remove from the heat, add the remaining chocolate and stir until smooth.

Working with one bacon slice at a time, dip the bottom half of the bacon into the chocolate and allow the excess to drip off. Holding the bacon over another bowl, scatter the sprinkles over the chocolate-coated area and place onto the prepared tray. Refrigerate for 20 minutes or until set.

Store in a sealed container in the refrigerator for 1–2 days.

Bacon donuts with chocolate cream

MAKES 15

500 g (1 lb 2 oz) plain baker's (strong) flour

300 ml (10 fl oz) full-cream (whole) milk

100 g (3½ oz) unsalted butter, chopped

1 free-range egg

2 tablespoons soft brown sugar

2 teaspoons dried yeast

1 teaspoon salt

canola or grapeseed oil for deep-frying

caster (superfine) sugar, to coat

15 slices Candied bacon (page 17)

Whisk 2 tablespoons of the flour with the milk in a heavy-based saucepan. Cook over medium heat, whisking constantly, until the mixture thickens and just comes to the boil. Remove from the heat and transfer to a large bowl. Whisk in the butter until melted and combined, and leave to cool to lukewarm, whisking occasionally.

Whisk the egg into the lukewarm milk mixture then add the remaining flour and the brown sugar, yeast and salt. Mix to form a soft dough, cover with plastic wrap or a damp cloth and set aside for 10 minutes.

Turn the mixture onto a lightly floured work surface and knead for 5 minutes or until quite smooth. Don't be tempted to add lots of flour, the dough will become less sticky as you knead it. Place the dough into a clean bowl. Cover and set aside in a warm place to prove for about 1 hour or until the dough doubles in size (the time will depend on the temperature).

Meanwhile, for the filling, combine the milk and vanilla extract in a medium heavy-based saucepan over medium heat and bring just to the boil. Remove from the heat and stir in the chopped chocolate. Beat the sugar and eggs in a large heatproof bowl with an electric mixer until thick and pale. Beat in the cornflour and cocoa. While still whisking, slowly pour the hot milk mixture into the egg mixture and whisk until combined. Clean the saucepan and return the mixture to the pan over medium heat. Cook, whisking constantly by hand, until the mixture thickens and just comes to the boil. Transfer the mixture to a large heatproof bowl and whisk in the bourbon, if using. Press a piece of plastic wrap over the surface to stop a skin forming

These pillowy donuts are stuffed full of oozy chocolate custard and topped off with crunchy candied bacon. These are definitely best devoured within a few hours of making them – not a difficult task.

CHOCOLATE CUSTARD FILLING

500 ml (17 fl oz/2 cups) full-cream (whole) milk

1 teaspoon natural vanilla extract

80 g (2¾ oz) dark chocolate, chopped

75 g (2¾ oz/⅓ cup) caster (superfine) sugar

2 free-range eggs

40 g (1½ oz/⅓ cup) cornflour

3 tablespoons Dutch-processed cocoa, sifted

2 tablespoons bacon-infused bourbon (optional)

NOTE: IF YOU FEEL LIKE AN EXTRA SMOKY BACON HIT IN THE FILLING, INFUSE THE MILK FOR THE FILLING OVERNIGHT WITH CHOPPED CRISP BACON AS PER THE ICE CREAM RECIPE ON PAGE 80.

and set aside to cool, whisking occasionally, then refrigerate for 1–2 hours until chilled. To cool quickly, whisk the filling in a bowl over an ice bath.

Turn the proved dough onto a lightly floured work surface. Knead the dough very gently for 5 seconds or until smooth. Rest the dough for 5 minutes. Pat the dough out into a circle about 1.5 cm (½ in) thick and cut out as many rounds as you can using a 7 cm (2¾ in) cutter. Place the rounds on a tray lined with baking paper, ensuring you leave at least 3 cm (1¼ in) space between them, and cover loosely with plastic wrap or a damp tea towel. Knead the remaining dough together gently, rest for a few minutes and cut more rounds. You should end up with about 15. Set aside in a warm place for about 30 minutes or until risen slightly.

Heat the oil in a deep saucepan or deep-fryer to 160°C (320°F). A cube of bread added to the oil will turn golden brown in 20 seconds. Add 2–3 donuts to the hot oil and cook for about 2 minutes each side or until puffed, golden brown and cooked through. Use a slotted spoon to remove and drain on paper towel. Repeat with the remaining rounds.

Toss the just-cooled donuts in the caster sugar to coat. Spoon the custard into a piping bag fitted with 5 mm (¼ in) nozzle. Push the nozzle into the centre of each donut through the side and pipe the custard into the donut until it feels heavy. Pipe an extra dollop of custard on top of each donut and top with candied bacon.

Close your eyes and imagine the best possible baking smell wafting through your kitchen, infused with sweet cinnamon and maple-banana. Now imagine a sizzling pan of bacon right in the middle of everything and you have yourself these delectable scrolls. Mouth. Watering ...

MAKES 12

500 g (1 lb 2 oz) plain baker's (strong) flour

350 ml (12 fl oz) full-cream (whole) milk

1 tablespoon maple syrup

50 g (1¾ oz) butter, melted, plus extra to serve

1 large free-range egg

2 teaspoons dried yeast

1 teaspoon salt

150 g (5½ oz) rindless loin (back) bacon, chopped

maple syrup, to glaze

BANANA-WALNUT FILLING

30 g (1 oz) butter, softened

55 g (2 oz/¼ cup) brown sugar

2 ripe bananas

1½ teaspoons ground cinnamon

1 teaspoon ground cardamom

45 g (1½ oz/⅓ cup) chopped walnuts or pecans

Whisk 2 tablespoons of the flour with the milk and syrup in a saucepan. Cook over medium heat, whisking, until the mixture thickens and comes to the boil. Remove from the heat, transfer to a bowl and leave to cool to lukewarm, whisking occasionally. Whisk the butter and egg into the lukewarm milk mixture then add the remaining flour, yeast and salt. Mix to form a soft dough, cover with plastic wrap and set aside for 10 minutes.

Turn the mixture onto a lightly floured work surface and knead for 5 minutes or until very smooth. Don't be tempted to add lots of flour, the dough will become less sticky as you knead it. Place the dough into a clean bowl. Cover and set aside in a warm place to prove for about 1½ hours or until the dough doubles in size (the time will depend on the temperature).

For the filling, beat the butter and sugar together in a bowl with a fork. Mash in the bananas and add the spices and nuts and a pinch of salt. Line a baking tray with non-stick baking paper. Turn the dough onto a lightly floured work surface and, without knocking all the air out of it, gently roll it out to a 30 cm x 40 cm (12 in x 16 in) rectangle. Gently spread the banana mixture over the dough and sprinkle with the bacon. Roll up firmly from one long side and, using a sharp knife, cut into 12 even slices. Place on the prepared tray, close together so they're almost touching, and cover loosely. Put the tray in a warm place for about 30 minutes or until dough has risen 2-3 cm (¾-1¼ in).

Meanwhile, Preheat the oven to 180°C/350°F (fan-forced). Bake for 15 minutes, then reduce the heat to 160°C/320°F (fan-forced) and bake for a further 10 minutes or until well-risen and golden. Brush or drizzle the tops of the warm scrolls with maple syrup and serve warm with butter.

Sticky maple syrup, bacon & banana scrolls

Cinnamon-spiced bacon monkey bread

SERVES 8-10

500 g (1 lb 2 oz) plain baker's (strong) flour

300 ml (10 fl oz) full-cream (whole) milk

100 g (3½ oz) unsalted butter, chopped

1 free-range egg

2 tablespoons soft brown sugar

2 teaspoons dried yeast

1 teaspoon salt

250 g (9 oz) trimmed rindless bacon, cut into 1 cm (½ in) dice

60 g (2 oz) butter, melted

Whisk 2 tablespoons of the flour with the milk in a heavy-based saucepan. Cook over medium heat, whisking constantly, until the mixture thickens and just comes to the boil. Remove from the heat and transfer to a large bowl. Whisk in the butter until melted and combined, and leave to cool to lukewarm, whisking occasionally.

Whisk the egg into the lukewarm milk mixture then add the remaining flour, sugar, yeast and salt. Mix to form a soft dough, cover with plastic wrap or a damp tea towel and set aside for 10 minutes.

Turn the mixture onto a lightly floured work surface and knead for 5 minutes or until quite smooth. Don't be tempted to add lots of flour, the dough will become less sticky as you knead it. Place the dough into a clean bowl. Cover and set aside in a warm place to prove for about 1 hour or until the dough doubles in size (the time will depend on the temperature).

Put the bacon in a large, cold heavy-based frying pan and cook over medium-high heat, stirring occasionally, for 6-8 minutes until well browned. Remove with a slotted spoon and drain on paper towel.

For the cinnamon spice coating, combine the ingredients in a small bowl. Set aside.

Generously grease a 22 cm (8¾ in) bundt tin.

Monkey bread is essentially cake made out of bunch of cinnamon donuts squished together. And the coating turns into a gooey, spiced caramelly bacony sauce as it bakes. Why am i still talking? Go make this right now!

CINNAMON SPICE COATING

150 g (5½ oz) soft brown sugar

2 teaspoons ground cinnamon

1 teaspoon mixed spice

Turn the proved dough onto a lightly floured surface. Knead the dough very gently for 5 seconds or until just smooth. Divide the dough into four even portions, and then roll each portion gently into a log shape. Rest the dough for 5 minutes. Cut each log into 10 even portions, to end up with 40 pieces of dough. Roll the portions into balls. Dunk each ball into the melted butter then roll in the cinnamon spice coating. Place in the prepared tin, layering the coated dough balls with sprinklings of bacon pieces (reserve 2 tablespoons of the bacon for sprinkling over the monkey bread to serve).

Cover loosely and set aside in a warm place for about 30 minutes or until risen slightly. Meanwhile, preheat the oven to 160°C/ 320°F (fan-forced).

Bake the monkey bread for 30–35 minutes until well-risen and golden. Remove from the oven and set aside to cool for 10 minutes, and then give the tin a sharp rap on the kitchen bench to loosen it. Carefully turn onto a serving plate and sprinkle with the reserved bacon pieces.

NOTE: MONKEY BREAD IS BEST EATEN WARM – IDEALLY NOT LONG AFTER ITS COME OUT OF THE OVEN WHILE THE COATING IS STILL STICKY AND AMAZING. JUST BE CAREFUL TO NOT BURN THOSE MONKEY FINGERS.

Fudgy choc-caramel bacon cookies

MAKES 16

150 g (5½ oz) rindless loin (back) bacon, finely chopped

125 g (4½ oz) butter, softened

220 g (8 oz) caster (superfine) sugar

1 teaspoon vanilla extract

1 large free-range egg

225 g (8 oz/1½ cups) plain (all-purpose) flour

35 g (1¼ oz) unsweetened (Dutch) cocoa powder

½ teaspoon baking powder

½ teaspoon salt

125 g (4½ oz) dark chocolate melts, roughly chopped

60 ml (2 fl oz/¼ cup) dulce de leche (see note)

Preheat the oven to 160°C/320°F (fan-forced). Line a large baking tray with baking paper.

Cook the bacon in a non-stick frying pan over medium heat for 6-8 minutes, or until browned and slightly crisp. Transfer to drain on paper towel.

Beat the butter and sugar together with an electric mixer until creamy. Beat in the vanilla, then the egg. Sift in the flour, cocoa, baking powder and salt. Stir well to combine. Mix in the chocolate melts, bacon and 2 tablespoons of the dulce de leche.

Divide the dough into 16 even portions. Shape the mixture into 5-6 cm (2-2½ in) rounds. Place on the prepared tray, allowing at least 4 cm (1½ in) between each. Make an indent in the centre of each cookie and fill with a good ¼ teaspoon of the dulce de leche. Bake for 18-20 minutes until firm. Cool on the tray.

These cookies are best eaten on the day they are made, but will keep in an airtight container for up to 3 days.

NOTE: DULCE DE LECHE IS MADE FROM CARAMELISED MILK AND IS AVAILABLE FROM GOURMET FOOD STORES AND SPANISH OR LATIN-AMERICAN GROCERS.

These cookies are gooey bites of bacony bliss.
Keep a jar of dulce de leche in your fridge
so you can whip up a batch of these whenever
a bunch of bacon-loving buddies drop by.

When you're making brownies, there's no need to mess around. Pack as much crunchy goodness as you can in there to contrast with the gooey fudgy cakey bit.

Double-choc stout, macadamia & candied bacon brownies

MAKES 16

170 g (6 oz) butter, roughly chopped

150 g (5½ oz) dark chocolate, roughly chopped

125 g (4½ oz) rindless loin (back) bacon, cut into 1.5 cm (½ in) strips

330 g (11½ oz) soft brown sugar

3 extra-large free-range eggs

125 ml (4 fl oz/½ cup) stout or other dark beer

150 g (5½ oz/1 cup) plain (all-purpose) flour

35 g (1¼ oz) Dutch-processed cocoa powder

½ teaspoon baking powder

150 g (5½ oz) white chocolate, roughly chopped

100 g (3½ oz) macadamia nuts, roughly chopped

Preheat the oven to 160°C/320°F (fan-forced). Grease and line a 20 cm x 30 cm (8 in x 12 in) slice tin with baking paper, extending the paper over the two long sides to help remove the cooked brownie.

Combine 150 g (5½ oz) of the butter and the chocolate in a medium heavy-based saucepan over low heat and stir until melted and smooth. Set aside to cool for 15 minutes.

Heat the remaining butter in a large heavy-based saucepan over medium heat. Add the bacon and cook, stirring, for 6-8 minutes until well browned and crisp around the edges. Remove with a slotted spoon and set aside.

Whisk the sugar, eggs and stout together in a large bowl, then whisk in the cooled chocolate mixture. Sift the flour, cocoa and baking powder into the bowl and add half of the white chocolate and half of the macadamias. Stir until just combined. Pour into the prepared pan and scatter with the remaining white chocolate and the macadamia nuts and bacon.

Bake for 30-35 minutes or until a skewer inserted in the centre comes out with just a few crumbs clinging to it. Allow to cool in the pan for 15 minutes before removing. Cut into pieces and enjoy warm and gooey or leave to cool. These brownies will keep in an airtight container for up to 3 days.

Maple-bacon indoor s'mores

MAKES 6

12 digestive biscuits (graham crackers)

peanut butter, to spread

100 g (3½ oz) dark chocolate, melted

MAPLE-BACON PRALINE

1 teaspoon olive oil

100 g (3½ oz) rindless loin (back) bacon, cut into 5 mm dice

2 tablespoons maple syrup

To make the maple bacon praline, first line a baking tray with baking paper. Heat the oil in a non-stick frying pan over medium-high heat. Cook the bacon for 6-8 minutes, stirring often, until well browned and crisp. Remove with a slotted spoon and drain on paper towel. Discard the rendered fat from the pan and return the pan to the heat with the bacon and the maple syrup. Cook, stirring, for 2-3 minutes until the maple syrup becomes sticky. Spread over the prepared tray and set aside to cool. Chop finely.

To make the maple bacon marshmallow, lightly spray an 18 cm x 28 cm (7 in x 11 in) baking tin with oil, line the base and two long sides with baking paper and lightly spray the paper with oil. Combine all but 2 tablespoons of the caster sugar with the maple syrup and 60 ml (2 fl oz/¼ cup) water in a medium heavy-based saucepan over low heat. Stir until dissolved. Bring to the boil and simmer, without stirring, until the syrup reaches 127°C (260°F) on a candy thermometer (move on to the following steps while the syrup comes to temperature, but keep a close eye on it).

Meanwhile, sprinkle the gelatine over 100 ml (3½ fl oz) cold water in a small microwave-safe bowl and set aside to absorb for 5 minutes. Zap in the microwave on high (100%) in 15-second bursts until the mixture is clear.

When the sugar syrup reaches about 115°C (239°F), whisk the egg white and remaining 2 tablespoons of caster sugar in an electric mixer on medium-high speed until thick and glossy. Reduce the speed to medium. When the sugar syrup reaches temperature (127°C/260°F), turn off the heat and set aside. Increase the mixer speed to medium-high and slowly pour the

The best thing about camping is toasting s'mores over the fire, right? Well, the smoky bacon here gives you that great campfire flavour without having to put up with sleeping on the ground or being eaten by bugs. Is there anything bacon can't do?

MAPLE-BACON MARSHMALLOWS

canola oil cooking spray

220 g (8 oz/1 cup) caster (superfine) sugar

3 tablespoons pure maple syrup

1 tablespoon glucose syrup

5 teaspoons powdered gelatine

1 large egg white

2 tablespoons icing (confectioners') sugar

2 tablespoons cornflour

gelatine liquid into the egg white mixture (be careful to not pour it on the whisk). Follow with the hot sugar syrup. Increase the speed to high and beat until the mixture is very thick, holds its shape and is cool to touch (8-10 minutes, depending on your mixer). Stir in the cooled maple bacon praline and immediately pour into the prepared tray. Smooth the surface with a spatula and set aside at room temperature for 1-2 hours until firm.

Combine the icing sugar and cornflour and dust the top of the set marshmallow. Turn out onto a clean chopping board and dust with more of the sugar-cornflour mix. Cut the marshmallow into 12 even-sized pieces with a long, lightly oiled knife and toss in the remaining coating mix, dusting off the excess. You'll only need six marshmallows to make the s'mores so store the remaining six for snacking on later in an airtight container in the refrigerator for up to 3 days.

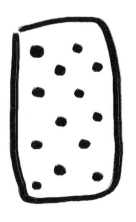

Spread all of the biscuits with a little peanut butter. Place the marshmallows on a tray lined with foil. Use a kitchen torch to toast the marshmallow on the top and sides. Top half of the biscuits with the toasted marshmallow, toasted side down. Toast the top of each marshmallow with the torch, drizzle with chocolate and sandwich with the remaining biscuits. Serve immediately.

NOTE: TRY MAKING BACON MARSHMALLOW POPS - CUT THE MARSHMALLOW INTO CUBES. INSERT LOLLIPOP STICKS AND DIP INTO MELTED DARK CHOCOLATE. ALLOW TO SIT UPRIGHT WHILE THE CHOCOLATE SETS. WRAP IN A CELLOPHANE BAG FOR A GREAT GIFT FOR THE BACON- INCLINED.

The zucchini in this recipe keeps these cupcakes dense and moist so they can compete with the tart and decadent cream cheese frosting and crunchy bacon sprinkles.

MAKES 12

335 g (12 oz/2¼ cups) plain (all-purpose) flour

2 teaspoons baking powder

½ teaspoon each bicarbonate of soda (baking soda), nutmeg and allspice

1 teaspoon ground cinnamon

pinch of salt

285 g (10 oz/1¼ cups) soft brown sugar

360 g (12½ oz/2 cups) finely grated zucchini

60 g (2 oz/½ cup) each chopped pecans and dried cranberries

3 large free-range eggs

250 ml (8½ fl oz/1 cup) mild oil

maple syrup, to drizzle (optional)

BACON SPRINKLES

2 teaspoons sunflower, rice bran or mild olive oil

125 g (4½ oz) rindless loin (back) bacon, finely chopped

MAPLE FROSTING

250 g (9 oz) cream cheese, softened

60 g (2 oz/½ cup) icing (confectioners') sugar, sifted

40 g (1½ oz) butter, softened

60 ml (2 fl oz/¼ cup) pure maple syrup

Preheat the oven to 160°C/320°F (fan-forced). Line a 12-hole muffin tray with paper cases.

Combine the flour, baking powder, bicarbonate of soda, spices, salt, sugar, zucchini, nuts and cranberries in a large bowl.

Mix the eggs and oil in another bowl and pour into the dry mixture. Stir until combined. Divide mixture the cases and bake for 25 minutes, or until springy to touch. Remove from the oven and transfer to a wire rack to cool completely.

Meanwhile, for the bacon sprinkles, heat the oil in a small frying pan over medium heat and cook the bacon for 2–3 minutes until very crisp. Drain on paper towel.

For the frosting, beat the cream cheese and butter together with an electric mixer until very smooth. Beat in the icing sugar then drizzle in the maple syrup and beat until combined and creamy.

Pipe or spread the frosting onto the cooled cakes. Scatter the bacon over the top and drizzle with more maple syrup if you like. These cupcakes are best eaten on the day they are made.

Spiced Zucchini Cupcakes
with bacon
sprinkles

Index

Published in 2018 by Smith Street Books
Collingwood | Melbourne | Australia
smithstreetbooks.com

ISBN: 978-1-925418-77-4

CIP data is available from the National Library of Australia

Publisher: Paul McNally
Senior editor & introductory text: Hannah Koelmeyer, Tusk studio
Recipe development: Caroline Griffiths & Jane O'Shannessy
Design concept & illustrations: Stephanie Spartels
Design layout: Heather Menzies, Studio31 Graphics
Photographer & Stylist: Billy Law

Printed & bound in China by C&C Offset Printing Co., Ltd.
Book 60
10 9 8 7 6 5 4 3 2 1

Please note: recipes in this book have previously appeared in
The Little Bacon Cookbook, published by Smith Street Books in 2016.

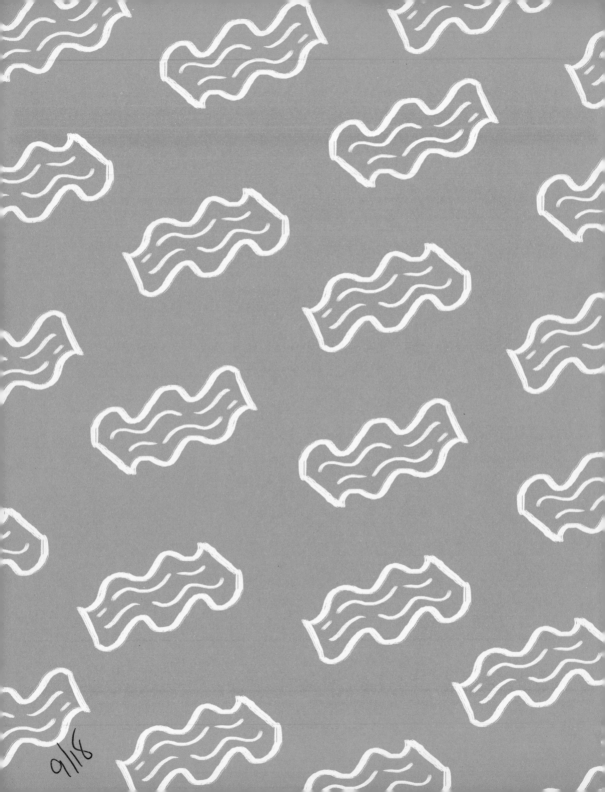

9/18